Light-headed

To andrea,
with love
Ruth ⊕ 2014.

Light-headed

Ruth Templeton

ATHENA PRESS
LONDON

ISBN 978 1 84748 717 9

First published 2010 by
ATHENA PRESS
Queen's House, 2 Holly Road
Twickenham TW1 4EG
United Kingdom

Printed for Athena Press

For my husband Wynford Lloyd Thomas

The Poems

Contents

Light-headed

I dream of a corpse. Do the dead call?
Spirit says, 'I deconstruct myself, fall
Into my fourteen sections, torn apart.'
Protoplasm seeps and floats out to sea.
'The wave and the sea are one.'

The goddess Maat weighs the dead heart,
Removes integument, like a serpent's skin.
The flame of love, a feather on the head,
Flutters around the trembling soul.

There will be poppies bleeding into corn
In acanthus, carnation and sweet pea.
For we are entwined with a golden thread
Circumscribed with pools of heat and breath,
Transformed into vibrating molecules
Full of the power, nowhere, the *nothing*
We set substance alight! And with Spirit see
A garland, with flowers of immortality.

Dylan Thomas

We could not take you into Sainsbury's,
Wobbling and unwashed,
Looking like and talking of death,
Rolling your eyes at the checkout.

So I said,
'Trees, stars, flowers',
Hoping to lift your spirit.

But your preoccupation
(vibrating the *r*, putting the emphasis on *pa*),
Your hollowness,
Was like a vacuum too deep to fill,
As if you had fallen into a
Deep well
And had lost the
Inclination to climb out.

Ariel

I lie upon the grass,
Look up at to the sky,
Hear the laughter of a couple
On the footpath nearby.

Thought becomes form
With strange presentiments.
Imagination shapes a sprite,
The air its element.

Homage to Spring

May I experience Him everywhere,
In beautiful blossom created from air.
Startling, blue, golden. He shines
Every morning. I am dazzled.
The earth sings, stung with green,
Luscious, silent, unfathomable, serene.

The evening twilight embraces a flower,
Growth is drenched in sentient power,
Concealed and concealing a darling dream,
A myriad of tremulous vibrations, seen
Ascending, caressing the spirit furled.
A wonderful agape holistic world.

Rescue in Piccadilly

Time and space, now and here. I see
My hands dancing in front of me.
Reflective and sad, my as yet unlined face.
I fret, lounging around this place
Overlooking Piccadilly.
I'm waiting to rescue another lost soul
With a drink problem he cannot control.

On my way here, a man in the rain
Stood forlorn on Surbiton bridge.
Mournful-eyed, he watched trains pass,
His skin tinged with jaundice,
Dressed in a shabby pea-green mac.
His expression had an appeal
Like the alcoholic bastard
For whom I have prepared a meal
While he spends my money on gin,
Roaming around London. My spirits sink.

Tremulous with drink, the comic
Has returned, jaunty from caprice.
For fun he puts my make-up on
And flutters his eyelashes obliquely
Smiling like Gloria Swanson –
His favourite drunken impersonation.

Alcoholism Sanctified

I witness your dark and drunken despair,
Violated, abused,
Clutching the air
As you fall down wretched, bruised.
It is dreadful to see you search for oblivion,
Pull your hair, beat the ground, cry, your face crumble.
I reach out to you and feel myself stumble.
You call any love a clumsy intrusion –
A travesty driven by confusion.

Florence in Hospital

In hospital Florence lingers
Like a withered oak, sad, broken.
Her breathing quiet, subdued
In silent accusation.

She is dying on starched white sheets. A stroke
Brought suffering, indignity.
Two hourly turns, over and over,
Visibly excite the nurses' pity.

Soap, ammonia, that faint stench
Of beds that have lost the human smell.
As in institutions long forgotten,
She is locked inside her private hell.

Zermatt

Near the campsite, where hope and faith unite,
The mean Matterhorn can be seen
Looming close, wrapped in silver cloud,
Like a translucent and immortal shroud.
A macabre profile smiles from its great height,
Observing all life, icy and serene.

Looking at the moss, rocks, Rhine and sky,
Strength comes to the heart and soul like food,
Eyes become topaz. Is it a dream or a magic spell?
A brief and breathless moment, then farewell.
Like sunlight shining on a butterfly,
The mountain remains a place of solitude.

Beefburger

We are cargo, herded close, separated from
Fodder, pasture, livestock, our smallholding,
The space of green fields, the light of the sun.

Crowded close we whine, we plead, we implore,
With eyes dilated, liquid with fear, we
Struggle, trapped between doors, walls, the floor.

Our journey lasts for ever. Time goes slow.
A part of me dismembers in this throng.
The sea is rough. My stomach heaves and oh!

Hopeless. If only I could be alone.
My heart in my hooves beats desolate,
Nostalgic for stable, aurochs and stone.

But, unable to understand, we ran
Past ruts, in pain, our flanks were hit with sticks,
Our journey just an economic plan.

Poem for a Winter's Night

As I walk in the moonlight,
There is a chill in the air,
The grass has a layer
Of silvery frost,
Each blade suspended,
Poised or lost
In terracotta stone.

I kick the dead leaves;
They sound like withered bone
Crunched underfoot in the cold.
The unrelenting night-time grips me
With a strange propitious hold,
Heavy with mystery.

Love sinks my heart to the depth of the sea,
Soars my soul to infinity –
Me and the night and the galaxy –
Until the wind howls
And disturbs this reverie
And I hurry home, to safety.

Actaeon

Actaeon ran with the moving earth,
His being transformed into a stag.
The land glittered and vibrated a cascade
Of aura that surrounded all phenomena.
He saw rotating forms and was afraid.
Running, running deep into the forest, breathless.
Hearing his own fearful breath, he ran in awe
Of movement in the mineral, vegetable and animal world.
Pressure builds up, breaks down, pulsates.
Creating relentlessly, bearing fruit and disintegrating.

Some Kind of Blessing

We are running wildly with a kite
Which fell to earth. In the light,
With patience, we unravel string,
Concentration unwavering.
The sky is high, there is no sound,
The kite is limp and on the ground.

Benedictine Monk

I travel, wear a fur coat. It's cold.
My ears pierced, straight dark long fine hair,
Red ankle-strap shoes, thick-soled,
Of limitations unaware.

He stood like any passenger,
I knew he was God's messenger.
The dining car provides the way
To capture his calm attention.
Grushenka, Alyosha K.

I smoked. We talked. His eyes were bright.
Creation. Being. Becoming.
Nathan warned King David, 'Tonight,
Be ready for Christ returning.'

I said I loved Dostoevsky.
He spoke of vows undertaken –
To be poor, chaste and to obey.
The train stopped. It was my station.
A different destination.

Matisse Speaks to Picasso

When trouble comes, you pray,
You do, you know. When things
Are bad, you throw away
All doubt and pray. God brings
Relief to sufferings.

Smokey Spanish Bar

He doesn't love her
So she screams and raves.
He says,
'Look, can we talk about this quietly?'
And the wine glass shaking in her hand
Glimmers in the early morning sun.
She runs outside into the icy air
Fragrant with sweet almond blossom,
Yells and stamps her foot and waves a fist
In his direction.

His hand has a slight tremor
His bluest-of-blue eyes blink and bleed into sclera,
He tries to smile and, speaking with a slight lisp
And Connecticut drawl,
He says,
'Consciousness is like clear water,'
Puts a large black hat on his head,
Turns, and walks away.

That night in the bar I could see
His thin face beneath a soft black hat.
He sighs.
'I think I'll go home early; I'm in the mood for suicide.'
But then he leans towards me
With a smile he tries to hide.

I think, his mould reminds me
That a head can balance exquisitely
Upon a neck. I look at his cornflower-blue eyes,
His shoulder blades and thighs.
Outside it is dark. Perfume from the flowers fills the air.
I look again, but he isn't there.

Humberside

I walked the dog by the turbid river,
Grey water laps over burnt-umber mud.
I see cars on the approach span to Hull.
The Humber Bridge suspension cable, solid
In the morning sun, touches the skyline.
The dog runs to search for lost canine friends,
Inclines his head to a distant train.
I shiver. The river flows. His bark blends
With cries of migrant birds. Autumn comes again.

Gravity

Speak to me of gravity
With myth or metaphor.
O, I fall, things slip away!
Down, down. Will Hathor restore
Earth, pull the moon close to her?

Shall I follow? Is it holy?
React? Wave my arms in the space
Where the lunar cycle takes place?
I descend. Hades' dark face
Awaiting Persephone.

Autumn in Sherwood Forest

I love yellow roses. Just being alive.
A Turner painting, Constable skies.
The cornflower-blue of inviolable eyes.

At my feet oak, birch, a variety of leaves.
I feel His presence in the breeze
In Sherwood, talking to the trees.

Yellow

It is ego, ouroboros and egg yolk;
It changes tomato juice pink.
It is choleric types and bilious folk,
A tiger lurking in my psyche when I think.
Chicken feathers and Sunday sun,
An Albers painting departing through a square
Into the tonal values of Vincent's sunflower
Infected cells, those lymphocytes
Flowing through lymph glands hour after hour,
It usually casts a purple shadow.
Six letters, two syllables, two Ls an O,
It reminds me of gravity, above, below.
It fills the buttercup and daffodil's head,
Tints the waxen skin of the dead,
Occupies the pain of Hephaestus' foot;
Superior to quicksilver, mercury-bright,
Though it dances in a shaft of sunlight
With the radiant force and beautiful glow.
It is an eagle, flying away,
Holding the thread of Ariadne.

Moving into Space

I move into a space of limitless extension
With my father, whose eyes, as he passed on,
Invaded my face. A place
Geometrically of power, force and form.
Divine circumscription in eternity pulsates
In a well-ordered cosmos of luminous stars.
Then he touched my heart to its deepest deep,
I felt like a wave with the sea below,
In a tapestry of fins, fingers and feet,
Strange and complete – an explosion of heat
As soul returned to spirit and let go.

Four Ashes

I travelled by ferry across the North Sea,
Watching the passengers above, below.
Seagulls fly above the stern, surround, follow
The boat. They cry. I wave my hand.
The birds will now return to land.
The ocean murmurs, 'Safe journey.'

Honesty Seeds

I imagine my lost ova
Soft and creamy with sentient power.
The texture of Japanese silk,
A purple iris flower.
They danced on the head of a pin,
Silhouetted in de Chirico space,
Then swam like a fish's fin
To sing in a heavenly place
And missed the race.

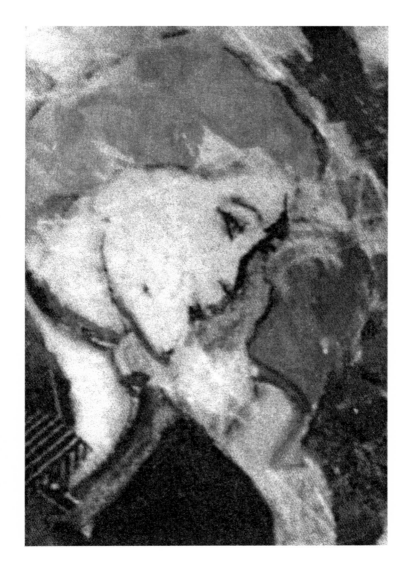

St James's Street Haikus

Pigeons
A sunny morning
Pigeons on the bird table
Eating the birdseed.

Blackberries
Purple blackberries
Sit frozen in the white bowl.
Sweet tastes the honey.

Ladybird
Ladybird on wall,
Black spots adorn her red wings,
Moved to green ivy.

Goldfish
It's never too late
For the goldfish in the bowl
To swim in the pond.

Old Man
Your beard is mangy,
How you have let yourself go,
Look, your shoes have holes.

Seagull
Will you scientists
Explain to me the seagull
Against the blue sky?

Black Holes
You smug scientists
Are creating a big bang
And making black holes.

Woodlouse
Can you understand
How a very small woodlouse
Curls into a ball?

Self-creators
Many friends need proof
That God is the creator.
They think they know best.

Science
You dissect the legs
Of the mysterious frog
With a hardened heart.

Dreadlock
Handsome young black youth
Wearing hair in dreadlock style
Smiles, serenely calm.

Pigeons
Pigeons hurry by,
They imagine food is near –
Are disappointed.

Talking
Words follow each word,
The mind is racing ahead.
Pause, friend, for a breath.

Stop It!
Stop this depression,
You are getting on my nerves.
Meditate, my friend.

Bo
I can see you shine
When you dance around the floor,
As the music plays.

Journey
Get ready to go,
Make steady progress, darling.
The train will leave soon.

Three Haikus at Night
Behind blue shadows,
The curved beam is still glowing,
From nights barely known.

Above the drifting
Scaly depths of the dark pool
A green crust glistens.

The stripped bones of trees
Make up a set memory;
They scorch the cool sky.

Orpheus

Propelled by a furious force in yellow light,
Orpheus enters the underworld's night.
Rejecting earth's freedom and full of woes,
His heart is steady; to his beloved he goes.
Though he thinks in his soul he is free,
He remembers her presence. O Eurydice!
The winds moan to form these songs,
Orpheus journeys to where he belongs.

He turns away from metaphors of stone,
Geometry as white as bone,
Moving in haste, a Dostoevsky pace,
Rich rage, deep-rooted, consuming his face,
Rosy with passion that hovers endlessly.
Hades beckons, salaciously but silently.
He considers the heavenly stars from every quarter.
In this semblance of order – the fragrance, air, texture
    and water –
Orpheus looks at his white knuckles, lacking the sun,
All that remains are the nodes of a skeleton.

November

The park is magnificent in autumn,
Pebbles gleam in the river and the trees
Swoon in their blanket of leaves.

Night and the moon swoops high,
Taken by God's hand and pushed
Graciously across the sky.

Starling and robin
And a sky the palest blue,
The self waiting within.

Ideas formed from words,
Rain falling on the yew tree
And dead leaves the shape of migrant birds.

Student Nurses Visit the Turkish Baths

Together we formed a bevy,
Some ashamed of their bodies
Being weighed in a public place.
Blushing now, hands hiding our faces,
We traipse to the steam room in a line,
Grateful when a voice calls, 'Time
You lot were out!' Dry heat is more
Than tender feet on burning floor
Can stand. We slump on a hot seat.
Ouch! Our bottoms feel the heat.
Like galloping horses perspire,
An icy plunge may cool the fire.
We swim and float in the water,
A massage next and then shower.

Imagination before Sleep

I imagined vast amber landscapes,
High purple dunes that undulate,
A desert expanse waiting to stagnate –
Rocks, thistle and cactus, silver and green,
Thirsty and verdant and vespertine.
There was one discernable shape.

A solitary robed figure
Near an old stone ruin
Was bowed, reflective, as if on the brink,
Stood waiting, becoming a blur.
As the sky from pale magenta and pink
Changed to blue, cerulean.

He had come from an ancient monastic cell,
A small dark place where spiders play.
Every day he kneeled to pray
And under the moon he rang a bell.
The night would change to indigo,
Then the wind would blow away
Footprints from the desert sands.
And I would wake to a new day.

Dialogue with Jane before she Died

Question:
If you could live your life just as you please,
Free from hate, confusion and disease,
What changes might create Heaven from Hades?

Answer:
No enemies. My friends would be shadows.
Anger, like quicksilver, flows
From house to ocean, dancing in rainbows.

The Winker

He watches as I board the train,
Sit down and prepare to read my book.
He knocks upon the windowpane,
Winks without a smile when I look.
Ignoring him, his knocks and stare persist.
The train moves away from his white-knuckled fist.

He watches as each day I catch the train,
Then one day gets inside the carriage nearby.
I see the skyline, trees, house, fence, grain,
Matter, form, radiation in the air,
Horses, cows, bridge, coal mine, river.
The winker sits waiting behind me somewhere.

Admiration of a Baby's Feet

I wrapped my hands around each foot and squeezed,
Watching the serene face that had lightly snoozed
In the sun. Those rays that urged Hephaestus to speak.
I pressed each warm sole against my cheek.

With his mother I marvelled at his eyes,
Wondering what strange incarnation belies
That glazed quiescence. We beamed on him,
Praising ten perfect toes and golden skin.

Autumn II

The sunlight was like burnished gold, draped over trees.
The fields, rich in gorse and daisies, dazzled.
From out of the shimmering, a white horse trots
To my beckoning, his friendly fetlock moves in the air.
I enjoy the shape of his mane
And look in his eyes, liquid and tame.

Snake

It is easy to slide along
A darkened hole and spit,
Narrow a jewelled eye, flick
A forked sharp tongue, ooze venom.
And I become ammonite,
My scaly limbless reptile coil
Pressed into ancient soil.
Flashing serpent hate to stalactite,
I crave to crush hot flesh to an idea.
Bitter juices tremor through my gut.
Spite! O delirious viper, Ophidia.

Lightning Source UK Ltd.
Milton Keynes UK
23 March 2010